LOVE STORY
Ryan O'Neal and Ali MacGraw

LOVE STORY
Ryan O'Neal and Ali MacGraw

Directed by Arthur Hiller
Paramount, 1970

'Love means never having to say you're sorry,' uttered by the heroine of *Love Story* was the romantic catch-phrase echoed by young couples all over America. In the midst of the Vietnam war, student unrest, Black Power, and the hippie movement whose credo was all-embracing love, the film's affirmation of good, old-fashioned romance caught the public imagination with its simple boy-meets-girl story set against a snowy New England backdrop. But it skilfully combined the old Hollywood standbys of love across class barriers and the death of one partner, with modern sexual and verbal explicitness. Instead of the classical beauty of the stars of the past, Ryan O'Neal and Ali MacGraw represented the new fashion in well-scrubbed, all-American good looks.

O'Neal was Oliver Barrett IV, son of an eminent and wealthy family. MacGraw was Jenny Cavilleri, daughter of a Catholic pastry cook. They meet while students, fall in love and marry. There is much nude grappling, with classical music on the soundtrack to denote tenderness. The soupier theme music written by Francis Lai was used to underline the moments of lyricism and drama. The couple's blissful relationship, often seen in soft focus and slow motion, fed a love-hungry young public. Despite some financial problems, happiness is complete until...

'What can you say about a 25-year-old girl who died?' Oliver asks at the beginning of the film, preparing the audiences for Jenny's coming death. Thus every moment the lovers have together is tinged with the knowledge of approaching tragedy. He begins to answer his own question. 'She loved Mozart, Bach...and The Beatles.' There she was immediately, a mixture of classicism, romanticism and modernism. Like the film itself. When Oliver discovers that hs wife is dying, he keeps it from her, although the brave girl knew all along. As Jenny dies, she urges her husband to have no regrets since she has none herself. As he leaves the hospital after her death, he runs into his father, who has disinherited him. When the father begins to apologise, Oliver repeats Jenny's definition of love.

The lovers-parted-by-death theme has several honorable antecedents. Greta Garbo expired in Robert Taylor's arms in *Camille* (1936), and Bette Davis died in *Dark Victory* (1939) as George Brent and audiences wept. Death was seen as an ennobling agent, the heroines becoming more radiant in its proximity. In *Love Is A Many-Splendored Thing* (1955), it is the man who dies. After William Holden is killed, Jennifer Jones continues to visit the verdant hill she associates with him. There was no tragedy in *Love Story*'s sequel *Oliver's Story* (1978), except at the box-office. Attitudes to romance had changed again and the greatest love stories seemed to be between a boy and his computer. At least the latter will not wrench the heart by dying of an incurable disease.

CONTENTS

LOVE STORY	5
FROM HERE TO ETERNITY	7
SOME LIKE IT HOT	9
ON GOLDEN POND	11
MOROCCO	13
ROMEO AND JULIET	15
CASABLANCA	17
AN AFFAIR TO REMEMBER	19
SON OF THE SHEIK	21
SUPERMAN	23
CLEOPATRA	25
LADY AND THE TRAMP	27
NOW VOYAGER	29
WITNESS	31
CAMILLE	33
FALLING IN LOVE	35
HIGH SOCIETY	37
GONE WITH THE WIND	39
TOP HAT	41
KING KONG	43
WUTHERING HEIGHTS	45
DOCTOR ZHIVAGO	47

INTRODUCTION

Love has always made the world of motion pictures go round. Whatever the Hollywood genre – western, *film noir*, epic or musical – love scenes are essential ingredients. Although pre-pubescent kids have been known to pelt the screen with popcorn during these close encounters of the romantic kind, more mature patrons expect and demand the moments when the hero and heroine's lips meet in closeup.

The first screen kiss can be accredited to May Irwin and John C. Rice in Thomas Edison's *The Kiss* (1896). It immediately provoked a gentleman to write, 'the spectacle of their prolonged pasturizing on each other's lips was hard to bear.' Despite this reaction, stars have 'pasturized on each other's lips' ever since. Three decades later, Greta Garbo and John Gilbert confimed that a love scene could be played lying down in *The Flesh And The Devil* (1927). In 1971, Bob Hope could say, 'The line "I love you" is no longer a declaration but a demonstration.'

Although films have become more explicit sexually, however, it is the power of romantic love that still has the strongest appeal for audiences. The far-ranging selection of films dealt with in this book proves that love in the cinema is a many varied thing. This even extends to the canine couple spooning anthropomorphically beneath the moon in Walt Disney's cartoon feature *Lady And The Tramp*, and the gigantic ape, *King Kong*, displaying non-bestial affection for the lightly clad Fay Wray screaming and squirming in his great palm. Doomed for other reasons than those which scotched the latter relationship is the 19th Century romance *Camille* ending with Garbo expiring in Robert Taylor's arms, a film which finds an echo in the contemporary tragedy of *Love Story*. Love sacrificed is represented by Humphrey Bogart waving farewell to Ingrid Bergman at the poignant end of *Casablanca*, and Harrison Ford leaving his Amish amour Kelly McGillis to her simple people as he returns to the big, bad city in *Witness*.

Love is also expressed in musical terms when Bing Crosby croons to the lovely Grace Kelly in *High Society*, and Fred Astaire and Ginger Rogers inimitably act out their emotions for each other as they fly across the dance floor in *Top Hat*. As *Superman*, Christopher Reeve literally takes his date Lois Lane (Margot Kidder) up among the clouds. Love-making ranges from Rudolph Valentino's macho treatment of Vilma Banky in *Son Of The Sheik* to Cary Grant's sophisticated courting of Deborah Kerr in *An Affair To Remember*. It includes the illicit grapplings of Burt Lancaster and an uncharacteristic Deborah Kerr on the beach in *From Here To Eternity*, as well as the tender moments Meryl Streep and Robert De Niro snatch away from their spouses in *Falling In Love*, while megastar couple Richard Burton and Elizabeth Taylor reflected their real-life love affair in *Cleopatra*. Septuagenarians Henry Fonda and Katharine Hepburn in *On Golden Pond* are no less touching in their love than the teenage 'star-crossed lovers' Leonard Whiting and Olivia Hussey as *Romeo And Juliet*. No matter what variations on the boy-meets-girl story there are, love is one of the cinema's most enduring themes, and continues to satisfy audiences' appetite for emotion and romance.

FROM HERE TO ETERNITY
Burt Lancaster and Deborah Kerr

FROM HERE TO ETERNITY
Burt Lancaster and Deborah Kerr

Directed by Fred Zinnemann
Columbia, 1953

Lush background music rises and breakers roll towards the shore as a lone couple make love after a swim on a deserted beach in Hawaii. Their mutual need finds a physical outlet in a passionate tumble on the sand. He is a First Sergeant restricted by army rules, which go against his rebellious nature. She is the frustrated and bored wife of an army captain, her ardent sexual desires having been repressed in what seems to have long been a loveless marriage.

Before they embrace, he reproaches her for having had previous affairs, which she reacts to defiantly. As they kiss, all the senses come into play. The feel of the sand on their wet bodies, the taste and smell of the salt spray, and the sound of the pounding waves. Finally, the soft lapping of the surf. Thus, the scene became one of the most vivid and talked about examples of sexual symbolism in the cinema, and the one that has been much parodied. Billy Wilder satirised it in *The Seven Year Itch* (20th Century-Fox, 1955) in which Tom Ewell daydreams that he is in a similar situation with Marilyn Monroe. Still part of movie mythology 27 years later, it was parodied as recently as in *Airplane* (Paramount, 1980).

The fact that the ardent adultress was played by Deborah Kerr, added a further *frisson* to the scene. The prim Miss Kerr, hitherto the epitome of well-bred English womanhood ever since her success in *The Life And Death Of Colonel Blimp* (1943), was clad in a nifty black one-piece bathing suit. Rescued from gentility, she grabbed the role, and the muscular Burt Lancaster, with both hands. But despite the daring (for 1953) beach games, her character was much toned down from that of the woman created in the James Jones bestselling novel, of which the film as a whole was a bowdlerised version. Nevertheless, the love scene stands out in sharp relief against the backdrop of corruption among the military, and the death and destruction to come in December 1941. For the film was set, and partially shot, in and around the Schofield Barracks at Pearl Harbor.

Contrasted with the unhappy wife on the beach, was the character of the prostitute (Donna Reed), called 'The Princess' because of her haughty attitude and her longing for respectability. Both Deborah Kerr and Burt Lancaster were nominated for Academy Awards but did not win any of the eight Oscars the picture received. Miss Kerr immediately resumed her adulterous doings in *The End Of The Affair* (Columbia, 1955) and got pregnant by married Lieutenant Colonel William Holden in *The Proud And The Profane* (Paramount, 1956), before resuming her ladylike ways in the musical *The King And I* (20th Century-Fox, 1956), playing the governess to the children of the King of Siam (Yul Brynner). She would let down her auburn hair from time to time in her career, but never with the same startling effect of that famous love scene on the beach.

SOME LIKE IT HOT
Tony Curtis and Marilyn Monroe

SOME LIKE IT HOT
Tony Curtis and Marilyn Monroe

Directed by Billy Wilder
United Artists, 1959

When Tony Curtis and Jack Lemmon disguised themselves in women's clothes in *Some Like It Hot*, they were not only carrying on an ancient comic tradition, but adding another aspect to the myriad facets of love on the screen. As seen later in *Tootsie* and *Victor/Victoria* (both 1982), drag creates a disturbing sexual ambiguity that goes beyond mere role playing or role reversal. There are, in fact, two love affairs in the movie. Joe (Curtis) and Jerry (Lemmon), jazz musicians on the run from gangsters in the Chicago of the 20s, join an all-girl band on its way to Florida. On the train, they become friends with Sugar Kane (Marilyn Monroe), the band's singer, with whom Joe falls in love. In Miami, Jerry/Daphne gets the unwanted attention of millionaire Osgood Fielding (Joe E. Brown), while Joe – when not masquerading as Josephine – woos Sugar in the guise of an oil tycoon.

In spite of the farcical plot, Billy Wilder's amalgam of parody, slapstick and romance has genuine emotion at its centre, especially in the figure of Marilyn's big-hearted, vulnerable, unlucky-in-love dumb blonde. She is one of life's eternal victims, taken in by men, and always ending up the loser. Two of her songs show the progression from hope to disappointment – 'I Wanna Be Loved By You' and 'I'm Through With Love', the latter rendition being provoked by Joe's having to leave her. He had taken on the persona of her ideal man – shy, bespectacled, intelligent, inexperienced with women and very wealthy – the opposite to his real self. As a finishing touch, he adds a Cary Grant accent. 'Nobody talks like that!' cries his friend Jerry.

Billy Wilder, who had never been able to procure the services of Cary Grant (whose transvestite peformance in *I Was A Male War Bride*, 1949, was an influence on the movie), transformed the screen's most debonair and self-assured lover into a near-sighted impotent being seduced by the ultimate sex goddess. The seduction scene, on Osgood's 'borrowed' yacht, has the woman on top of the man, attempting every artifice to defrost his frigidity. One of the first signs of her success are when his glasses begin to steam up. 'I spent six months in Vienna with Professor Freud, flat on my back,' he explains. 'Have you tried American women?' Sugar asks with typically Marilyn, wide-eyed innocence.

At the same time on shore, a tango in reverse is being performed by 'Daphne' and Osgood, in which the 'woman' assumes the dominant role. 'Daphne, you're leading again,' says Osgood. Jerry in his blonde wig, high-heel shoes and flapper's frock, has begun to identify more and more with his female guise. 'I will never again find a man so good to me,' he tells Joe with some truth. When Jerry becomes engaged to Osgood, he finally admits he is a man. Osgood, in one of the most memorable punchlines in the cinema, replies, 'Well, nobody's perfect.' If that isn't love, nothing is!

Lemmon and Joe E. Brown

Curtis and Monroe

ON GOLDEN POND
Henry Fonda and Katharine Hepburn

ON GOLDEN POND
Henry Fonda and Katharine Hepburn

Directed by Mark Rydell
Universal, 1981

'Working with Henry [Fonda] brings tears to my eyes,' said Katharine Hepburn while on location for *On Golden Pond*. 'He is so sensitive, so giving an actor. I've always admired him, of course, but working with him for the first time is a marvel.' Henry Fonda was equally excited about working with her. As a mark of Katie's affection for Fonda, she gave him an old hat that had belonged to Spencer Tracy. In return, Henry painted a picture of the hat for her. If they had come together sooner, their partnership might have filled the void left by the end of the famous Tracy-Hepburn era.

The extra-special chemistry between Spencer Tracy and Katharine Hepburn on screen reflected their devoted real-life romance, which they carried on discreetly from 1942 until his death in 1967. A devout Catholic, Tracy would never divorce his wife, former stage actress Louise Treadwell, although they had lived separately for many years. The story goes that when Spence and Kate were introduced on *Woman Of The Year* (MGM, 1942), the first of nine movies they made together, she said, 'I'm afraid I'm a little tall for you, Mr Tracy.' He replied, 'Don't worry, I'll soon cut you down to size.' Most of their films were witty battles of the sexes, with Katie invariably pretending to lose in order to keep her man. As the ad line read for *Adam's Rib* (MGM, 1949), one of their best pictures, they were 'the hilarious answer to who wears the pants.'

Hepburn and a seriously ill Tracy, were reunited for the last time in *Guess Who's Coming To Dinner?* (Columbia, 1967). He courageously managed to complete the film before dying a few weeks later aged 67. When both Hepburn and Tracy (posthumously) were up for Oscars for the film, she telephoned her maid in Hollywood, while on location in France, to find out if she had won her second Academy Award. 'Did Mr Tracy win it, too?' she asked. 'No, ma'am.' 'Well, that's okay, I'm sure mine is for the two of us.'

Henry Fonda, however, although ill and in hospital, was alive to receive his only Oscar for *On Golden Pond*, collected for him by daughter Jane, who was also in it. (It was Hepburn's fourth.) Some of the loving rivalry of the earlier partnership survived into the later one. Fonda, aged 75 and on a pacemaker, played Norman Thayer, an irascible retired professor just about to celebrate his 80th birthday. Hepburn was Ethel, his supportive wife, who puts up with his cantankerous moods because she knows he is dying. They bicker amiably enough, until Norman has a heart attack. The near-death scene, as he clings desperately to life and to his wife, proves that they are irrevocably in love. The poignancy was increased by the knowledge that Fonda died only four months after the film's release. The picture proved, in an industry – and in an era – where the affairs of teenagers and glamorous couples in their prime filled the screens, that love (and even sex) is not, in fact, the monopoly of the young.

Woman Of The Year (inset: *On Golden Pond*)

MOROCCO
Gary Cooper and Marlene Dietrich

MOROCCO
Gary Cooper and Marlene Dietrich
Directed by Josef von Sternberg
Paramount, 1930

One of the great legends of the cinema tells of how Josef von Sternberg took a plump *fraulein* and transformed her into the illusory vision of Eternal Woman. This glamorous *femme fatale* was Marlene Dietrich, who appeared in his films in different guises of the same spirit: Lola Lola (*The Blue Angel*, 1930) Amy Jolly (*Morocco*, 1930), Spy X27 (*Dishonored*, 1931), Shanghai Lily (*Shanghai Express*, 1934), Catherine the Great (*The Scarlet Empress, 1934)*, and Concho Perez (*The Devil Is A Woman*, 1935). Together, director and star created some of the most exotic, bizarre, libidinous and fanciful films ever made. The absurd plots, whether colonial adventure, spy mystery or historical romance, the dreadful dialogue delivered at a languorous pace by stereotyped characters – all were transformed by pictorial splendour and Marlene's mysterious beauty. She inhabited a phantasmagoric Morocco, Spain, Russia or China, all conjured up by the artistic and technical wizards on the Paramount backlot.

In one of the immortal examples of the Dietrich-Von Sternberg art, *Morocco*, eroticism was more implicit than explicit. Playing a cabaret singer, Dietrich donned male attire – top hat and tails – and sang 'What Am I Bid For My Apples?' to an audience which included Legionnaire Gary Cooper. She flirts with him outrageously, using her eyes beneath pencilled-in brows, while teasingly and ambiguously kissing a girl at a table. He appears in her dressing room after the show, hoping for the kind of affair he enjoyed with her predecessor, but duly finds himself becoming a moth around her flame. Eventually, he puts the Legion before his love for her. In the final sequence, Marlene is interrupted at dinner by the sound of the Legionnaires' departure. Nervously, she breaks a string of pearls and runs frenziedly after her lover. In a famous scene of high camp, she walks off into the desert to follow him, gradually discarding her high heels. How much more effective than the traditional climactic clinch!

By contrast, Marlene meets her old flame, Clive Brook, on board the *Shanghai Express* and, in a spirit of cynicism and implied reproach, tells him that 'It took more than one man to change my name to Shanghai Lily.' Leaning against a door, exhaling clouds of cigarette smoke, she reminds the stiff English army officer of their past love as he struggles to resist her. Like Cooper's Legionnaire, Brook is afraid that love will rob him of his independence, but everything conspires against him – the train, the landscape, the sexual jealousy aroused in him by the Chinese Warlord who holds them hostage, the fabulous costumes designed by Travis Banton – all serve to accentuate Marlene's desirability. She is at one and the same time a superb mask and a breathing sensuous woman. In the end Brook surrenders, relinquishing his officer's gloves and whip to her embracing grasp as they exchange a passionate kiss, to the envy of cinemagoing men the world over.

Shanghai Express (inset: *Morocco*)

ROMEO AND JULIET
Leonard Whiting and Olivia Hussey

ROMEO AND JULIET
Leonard Whiting and Olivia Hussey
Directed by Franco Zeffirelli
Paramount, 1968

Naturally, Shakespeare's *Romeo And Juliet*, the world's most enduring love story, has been filmed many times. As *Time* magazine put it, 'the play...has always been, the best version ever written of Hollywood's favourite theme, Boy Meets Girl.' But for the actors and actresses who have essayed the roles of the 'star-crossed lovers', there 'never was a story of more woe, than this of Juliet and her Romeo.'

In 1916, Harry Hillaird and Theda Bara for Fox and the (secretly) married couple, Francis X. Bushman and Beverly Bayne for Metro appeared in truncated, ludicrous silent films. In 1936, MGM's production chief Irving G. Thalberg was determined to have his wife Norma Shearer portray Juliet. 'I believe Norma can play anything and do it better than anyone else,' said the adoring hubby. Shearer took on the role of the 14-year-old Juliet at the age of 36, while her Romeo, Leslie Howard, was pushing 44. Howard at first refused saying, 'If he is as young as Romeo is reputed to be, we do not take him seriously. And if he is as old as the average actor has to be to have the necessary experience for this role, he is a bore.' Even so, the lavish production got generally good reviews.

In the 1954 version, freely adapted by the director Renato Castellani, the beautiful beginning of the balcony scene, 'But soft, what light from younder window breaks?', was cut in order to get on with the romantic business in hand. It was the first Technicolor production, and was handsomely photographed in and around Verona. But the performances from the too coldly enunciating Laurence Harvey and the inexperienced Susan Shentall made it more of a disaster than a tragedy. At least they both had the advantage of being in their early twenties, for which one remains thankful.

At last, in 1968, a genuine attempt was made to capture the fervour, intensity and poignancy of the young lovers, as intended by their creator. Franco Zeffirelli cast 17-year-old Leonard Whiting and 15-year-old Olivia Hussey in a film bustling with energy and colour, and the two leads were touchingly youthful in the first meeting at the Capulet's ball, during the balcony scene (almost intact), and after their secret marriage. In bed, Romeo shown completely nude and Juliet skimpily draped, gave the wedding night scene the eroticism implied in the play and notably missing from earlier versions. In fact, they could well have been kids of the 60s who had eloped. Unfortunately, in the later tragic scenes, the young stars provide to be inadequate, killing the verse long before they killed themselves.

Modern variations on this classic of doomed love have surfaced periodically, most notably *Les Amants De Verone* (*The Lovers Of Verona*, 1948) starring Anouk Aimee and Serge Reggiani, Leonard Bernstein's brilliant musical transformation to the slums of New York in *West Side Story* (1961), and the ballet version with Nureyev and Fonteyn.

The 1966 ballet version (inset: the 1936 MGM production)

CASABLANCA
Humphrey Bogart and Ingrid Bergman

CASABLANCA
Humphrey Bogart and Ingrid Bergman

Directed by Michael Curtiz
Warner Bros., 1942

The chemistry of Humphrey Bogart's partnership with his wife Lauren Bacall, both on screen and off, has become a legend in the chronicles of Hollywood romance. When Howard Hawks paired them for the first of their four films together, *To Have And Have Not* (Warner Bros., 1944), he told Bogart, 'You're the most insolent man on the screen and I'm going to make the girl a little more insolent than you are.' In fact, the picture showed a rare pairing of equals, with sultry Bacall on a par with rough-hewn Bogart in toughness, repartee and sexuality. Their entire screen relationship is encapsulated in the scene where she arrives in his room to seduce him. Before leaving, Bacall gives him 'The Look' and delivers the classic lines, 'You don't have to act with me Steve. You don't have to say anything or do anything. Maybe just whistle. You know how to whistle, don't you, Steve? You just put your lips together and blow.'

This was only the beginning, but for devotees of screen love affairs, the impact of Bogart and Bacall gives way before the memory of his pairing with the limpid Swede, Ingrid Bergman, in what must surely be the screen's most celebrated love story – *Casablanca*.

'Play it once Sam, for old time's sake. Play it Sam…' Sam (Dooley Wilson) starts tickling the ivories and singing 'As Time Goes By', as a quite radiant Ingrid Bergman listens enraptured. They are interrupted by the owner of the bar, Bogart. 'I thought I told you never to play it…' Then he sees her, his lost love. The tune is redolent of their idyllic few days together in Paris, before the war separated them.

The wonderfully orchestrated scene turns *Casablanca* from an adventure movie into a love story. Amidst the suspense and intrigue in the wartime Moroccan city, two people cling to the remembered moments of their shared past and ponder on the future. The reappearance of Bogart's old flame has opened old wounds. 'Of all the gin joints in all the towns all over the world, she walks into mine', he says in drunken self-pity. A flashback sees the lovers in Paris, just before the war, driving up the Champs Elysees. After dancing in a nightclub, he asks if there is another man in her life, breaking their arrangement to ask no questions of each other. 'I'm sorry for asking', he says, and offers the most well-known toast in movie history, 'Here's looking at you kid!' Back to the present, he knows that she is married to a resistance fighter (Paul Henreid) who needs a visa to the USA to escape capture. Bogart is the only man who can help, and Bergman is dependent on him. Although cynical, Bogart is soft-hearted and, in the end, Bergman flies to safety with her husband leaving Bogie, the man she still loves, watching from the runway. The poignant relationship created by the two stars has never been eclipsed on screen. It belongs uniquely to *Casablanca* which, as time goes by, looks better and better.

Casablanca

To Have And Have Not

AN AFFAIR TO REMEMBER
Cary Grant and Deborah Kerr

AN AFFAIR TO REMEMBER
Cary Grant and Deborah Kerr

Directed by Leo McCarey
20th Century-Fox, 1957

An ocean voyage is a notoriously romantic setting in which a love affair can flower. Often, though, it blossoms on the high seas, only to wilt later on land. The most famous of shipboard romances in the cinema was that of Charles Boyer and Irene Dunne in *Love Affair* (1939), reprised in CinemaScope and DeLuxe Color by Cary Grant and Deborah Kerr in *An Affair To Remember*. Made by the same director, Leo McCarey, and with the identical plot, both films managed to shift from light romantic comedy in the first half to tragic pathos in the second with consummate skill. The main appeal of what is basically a boy-meets-girl story, lies in the sensitive portrayal of how two sophisticated and jaded people come to discover the experience of actually falling in love.

There is little to choose between the graceful playing of the two couples in the different versions of the durable material. Each was able to produce both laughter and tears from an audience. Charles Boyer was the great continental lover of the 30s and 40s, at the same time as the Anglo-American Grant was romancing some of Hollywood's most glittering female stars. Almost 20 years later on, his light undimmed at the age of 53, Grant was in the arms of the ladylike red-haired beauty Deborah Kerr. Jerry Wald, producer of *An Affair To Remember* said, at the time, that 'The reason there are so few love stories being made, is that there are so few actors who could play them convincingly. Today's actors either look good and talk lousy or they look lousy and talk good. Cary Grant looks good and talks good'.

Often on the wide CinemaScope screen in the late 50s, fat closeups of lovers kissing tended to be rather overpowering or lacking in subtlety. McCarey depicts the first kiss between Grant and Kerr by revealing only their legs on one of the luxury liner's stairways. The rest of their affair is treated in a similarly discreet manner, as they are both pledged to others waiting to meet them in New York when the ship lands after its trans-Atlantic crossing via Naples.

In both pictures, the couple on board begin a flirtation to pass the time, not imagining that any deeper involvement might follow. As the ship steams across the ocean, however, so their love strengthens. On arrival in New York they are forced down to earth with a bump, but to test their love they resolve to meet again in six months at the top of the Empire State Building (a favourite rendezvous for metropolitan sweethearts in the movies). On the appointed day he arrives but on her way to the meeting she is involved in a car crash and is left a cripple. By chance, they meet again, she determines to learn to walk, and they look forward to a happy life ever after. The screenplay, the acting and the sensitive direction kept everybody's head above treacle level, and cinemagoers in the 30s and 50s got a sophisticated comedy and a superior soap opera all for the price of one ticket.

An Affair To Remember (inset: *Love Affair*)

SON OF THE SHEIK
Rudolph Valentino and Vilma Banky

SON OF THE SHEIK
Rudolph Valentino and Vilma Banky

Directed by George Fitzmaurice
United Artists, 1926

Son Of The Sheik was released opportunely by United Artists at the same time as the funeral of Rudolph Valentino, 'the screen's greatest lover', during which thousands of his grieving female fans caused a near riot. The film, a sequel to *The Sheik* (1921), told of the Arab-garbed Valentino's romance with nomadic dancer, Vilma Banky. 'Who are you my lord?' she asks in intertitles, 'I do not know your name.' 'I am he who loves you. Is not that enough?' he replies. Thus began the sado-erotic love scene that caused women's hearts to flutter at the sight of the famous male vamp.

Valentino has brought Banky to his tent, and begins kissing her suggestively along her arm and shoulder. He then forces her down upon a divan, his eyes glowing with lustful intent. Lighting a cigarette, he strips off his robe and unbuckles his jewelled belt. Her fear is plainly mingled with desire. 'I may not be the first victim but, by Allah, I'll be the one you remember!' The sheik then decides to reject her as she clings pleadingly to his legs. There is a huge close-up of her widening eyes. He seizes her in his arms and crushes her with kisses, driving her backwards towards the divan again. We do not see what happens next, but the wind blowing outside the tent reflects the tempest within. Later, captured and tortured by his enemies, he believes she has betrayed him, but he soon learns that she really loves him, and they ride off together to his sheikdom and, presumably, married bliss.

Valentino first emerged as the great 'Latin Lover' in *The Sheik*, more primitive (in a cinematic sense) than its sequel. The publicity shrieked, 'He wanted one thing and she knew what it was, and it would only be a matter of time before he got it.' As in the later film, male and female were alone in an isolated tent in the desert, but that time it was Agnes Ayres who was abducted. 'Why have you brought me here?' she demands. 'Are you not woman enough to know?' he replies. In a short time, the lovely Miss Ayres has exchanged her riding breeches for a skirt, revealing her femininity. When he kisses and embraces her, she coos, 'I am not afraid with your arms around me, Ahmed, my desert love, MY SHEIK!' The morning after, she is seen in her own tent, making it clear to audiences that nothing took place. Their liaison is further legitimized when Valentino reveals himself to be a Scottish nobleman, abandoned in the Sahara as a baby.

However clearly nonsensical the situations in his films might have been, Valentino did offer a taboo fantasy male to women among the predominance of female sex symbols on the screen. But it was essentially a safe image because, after the unmistakable suggestions of rape, abduction and slavery, Rudy usually settled for marriage. Valentino, who brought passion into the lives of millions of women who identified with Vilma Banky and Agnes Ayres, died unromantically of a perforated ulcer at the early age of 31.

The Sheik (inset: *Son Of The Sheik*)

SUPERMAN
Christopher Reeve and Margot Kidder

SUPERMAN
Christopher Reeve and Margot Kidder

Directed by Richard Donner
Warner Bros., 1978

Behind the corny comic book heroics of the Superman movies lies the assumption that within every shy, fumbling male, a Man of Steel is bursting to get out, and that this muscle-bound and righteous hero is exactly what the average woman dreams about. Someone literally to sweep her off her feet. However, statistics suggest that the modern girl is more likely to fancy the weakling who gets sand kicked in his face than the Charles Atlas type. The films gave Christopher Reeve the chance to appear as both sides of the masculine coin, although the well-named Margot Kidder as Lois Lane prefers the strong and protective Superman to Clark Kent, his mild-mannered, bespectacled other self. Like other dual personalities such as The Scarlet Pimpernel and Zorro, who also had effete alter egos, Kent becomes his own rival for the affections of the heroine.

When Clark Kent comes to work on *The Daily Planet* in Metropolis, he is immediately smitten by the slick, brisk and ambitious reporter Lois, but she fails to pay much attention to him. After Superman, a knight in shining red cape and blue tights, flies up and catches her in his safe and massive arms as she falls from a skyscraper, she then falls for him in a more figurative manner. Neglecting the love-lorn Kent even further, this knowing now-girl follows the traditional romantic line of rescued damsel swooning for an air-borne Lancelot in leotards. Lois obtains an exclusive interview with the Caped Crusader at her penthouse, and after some innuendo about his size, and the fact that he can see what colour panties she is wearing because of his X-ray eyes, Superman suggests she 'come fly with him'. Hand in hand, they leap off the balcony and go for a joyride in the sky, soaring amorously over the city at night, as she recites the lyrics of the love song, 'Can You Read My Mind?' It is the apotheosis of the romantic 'walking on air' feeling of couples, a touching and unique gravity-defying cinematic love scene.

More down-to-earth, and subverting the comic strip legend, Lois discovers the secret identity of her romantic hero in *Superman II* (1980). They want to get married but, due to the laws of Krypton, Superman is forbidden human love. He therefore renounces his superhuman powers and spends a rhapsodic night with Lois. But he then realises that his more primal need is to right the world's wrongs and so decides to sacrifice his own feelings. Thus Superman regains his strength, erases any memory of their love from Lois' mind and flies off to conquer evil as he had conquered love.

Endless Freudian interpretations are possible of what is superficially an enjoyable fairy tale, a wish-fulfilment fantasy in which the conception of a hero who can right all wrongs, is taken to its logical extreme. But like all such heroes, on screen or off, he is humanized by the fact that he can still give his heart to a woman.

Superman II (inset: *Superman*)

CLEOPATRA
Richard Burton and Elizabeth Taylor

CLEOPATRA
Richard Burton and Elizabeth Taylor

Directed by Joseph L Mankiewicz
20th Century-Fox, 1963

'Good Lord, the reputations we had. I mean, I was a bestial wife stealer and Elizabeth was a scheming home breaker. You'd think we were out to destroy Western civilisation or something,' said Richard Burton about his celebrated love affair with Elizabeth Taylor during the shooting of *Cleopatra*. Never had the personal relationship between two movie stars created quite so much public curiosity and ballyhoo. Of course, there had been other great lovers whose romance off-screen added to their interest on-screen – Garbo and Gilbert, Bogart and Bacall – but not to the giddy extent of Burton and Taylor. Their affair was followed like a real-life soap opera, their films considered merely reflections of it.

It all began on the set of the $40 million epic. The romantic entanglement between the ravishing 29-year-old Taylor (twice divorced, once widowed, and currently married to Eddie Fisher) and the 37-year-old Burton, then married to Sybil Williams, the mother of his two children, was well-documented in the purple prose of the world's press. 'I love Liz, but marriage is out. Liz and I aren't made for marriage. She has not had much luck in her love life and, apart from me, she hasn't known any real men.' By the end of the lengthy shooting, they were together.

The four-hour movie followed the plots of both Shaw and Shakespeare's plays on the Egyptian queen's affairs with Julius Caesar (Rex Harrison), and his ostensible successor, Mark Antony (Burton). After the elderly man-young woman relationship with Caesar, the Serpent of the Nile entwines herself around Antony, using her beauty, charm, wit and kohl-laden eyes. But the public were disappointed that the love scenes between Taylor and Burton that were the talk of modern Rome, were not repeated with quite as much passion in those of ancient Rome!

Public interest in the private life of Burton and Taylor made them into the highest paid couple in the movies, averaging a million dollars per picture. The publicity which accompanied their cycle of marriage, divorce, remarriage, and redivorce, kept audiences interested in seeing them together on the screen in the eleven, somewhat variable, films they made together. Burton earned his money by walking through his roles with a hangdog expression on his handsome, rather debauched features, while his wife looked glamorous. People felt they were getting an insight into their actual relationship when watching the pair duel raucously as a disenchanted married couple in *Whose Afraid Of Virginia Woolf?* (1966), tempestuously in *The Taming Of The Shrew* (1967), and uncomfortably in the TV drama *Divorce His, Divorce Hers* (1972). However, despite the vicissitudes of their romance, a genuine love kept drawing them together again, something the public recognised and warmed to. After all, everybody loves lovers, especially when they're larger than life.

The Taming Of The Shrew (inset: *Cleopatra*)

LADY AND THE TRAMP

LADY AND THE TRAMP

Directed by Hamilton Luske, Clyde Geronimi and Wilfred Jackson
Buena Vista, 1955

When two lovers kiss on the screen, an illusion of flesh and blood is created by the flickering celluloid image, although it has not much more reality than if the characters had been fashioned by a skilful artist. Ink and paint in the veins of cartoon creations does not prevent them from feeling romantic or displaying eroticism. Indeed, so sexy was Max Fleisher's Betty Boop, the saucer-eyed teasing flapper of animated pictures, that the Hays Office censored her in 1935, claiming she was 'immoral'. Popeye, the pipe-smoking, spinach-eating sailor with the mountainous biceps, who also popped out of Fleisher's ink well, usually fought to rescue his string-bean girlfriend from a fate worse than death. Walt Disney's purer images of womanhood such as Snow White, Cinderella and Sleeping Beauty dreamed that their princes would surely come one fine day. In each case, the idealized handsome man of their dreams swept them off towards happy-ever-after land, the same land where dwelt multitudes of characters portrayed by the romantic Hollywood stars.

However, amorous relationships among cartoon figures is not confined to human representations. Animal couples, such as Porky and Petunia Pig, Donald and Daisy Duck, and Mickey and Minnie Mouse, although not exactly Romeos and Juliets, have had their fair share of romance. Disney's *Lady And The Tramp* took the anthropomorphic to its furthest degree, the romance between the pretty cocker spaniel and the pleasant-looking mongrel closely echoing a traditional love story. Thus the plot follows the pattern of dog meets dog, dog loses dog, dog gets dog. Based on the premise that all dogs are equal, Lady, the pampered pet from Snob Hill falls for Tramp, a mutt from the wrong side of the tracks.

As their romance blossoms, Tramp shows the hitherto sheltered Lady something of his footloose and fancy free existence. One night, to impress her, he takes his sweetheart to the back door of an Italian Restaurant. Tony, the owner, and Joe, the cook, make a fuss of them as they would of any young couple in love. 'You take-a Tony's advice and settle down with this-a one,' Tony effuses. After serving their four-legged clients a meal of spaghetti and meat balls, Tony and Joe serenade them both with 'Bella Notte', a love song, accompanying themselves on accordion and violin. During the ditty, the canine couple nibble at the same strand of pasta, bringing their lips together in a kiss. When the serenaders sing of 'stars in her eyes', stars light up in Lady's large, brown eyes in a literal interpretation of lyrics as the camera pans up towards the moon. Then an off-screen chorus picks up the melody as background to a sequence of romantic vignettes, ending with the adoring doggies in Lovers' Lane admiring the full moon in mimicry of the human couples around them. Strangely, the love of Lady and Tramp, seemed no less valid for being felt by dogs, and cartoon dogs at that.

NOW, VOYAGER
Paul Henreid and Bette Davis

NOW, VOYAGER
Paul Henreid and Bette Davis

Directed by Irving Rapper
Warner Bros., 1942

'And will you be happy, Charlotte?' 'Oh, Jerry, don't let's ask for the moon. We have the stars.' Max Steiner's throbbing music swells, the camera pans up to the jewelled heavens, and audiences raise handkerchiefs to their eyes at the end of *Now, Voyager*. In the final transcendent moment, wartime audiences realised they would have to make the most of what fleeting happiness they could find and that 'it was better to have loved and lost, than never to have loved at all.'

It was a shimmering wish-fulfilment fantasy, in which a plain and introverted spinster blossoms into an assured and attractive woman, bringing hope to millions like her. All one needs for the transformation is a kindly psychiatrist to give one confidence, and a Continental lover in a white suit to bring it about. It is the fairy tale reversed where the prince kisses the frog, who turns into a beautiful princess; Cinderella for mature adults. However, the strict moral code of the era did not permit Charlotte to live happily ever after with her architect lover. She must remain, forever suffering, in a small compartment of his life, while he devotes most of his time to his unloved and unloving wife.

Bette Davis, never a glamour girl or associated with great romantic roles, played the soap opera for real, making the transition from Ugly Duckling to Swan extremely convincing. At the beginning, she is overemphatically homely and stout in a hideous Foulard dress with a heavy pattern, thick shoes, great beetling eyebrows, and glasses. Miraculously, she emerges on a South American cruise as slim and alluring, and with her poor eyesight cured. At first, hats shadow her face, suggesting shyness, but as she gets to know Paul Henreid as Jerry, the veil lifts from the face of Charlotte Vale.

One night, after dining in a restaurant overlooking a bay, they move out onto a patio. It is here that Henreid created an erotic tremor by lighting two cigarettes at the same time and handing one of them to her. The action, which set a new trend in lovers' smoking habits, is repeated twice more in the film to recapture this sublime romantic moment. Everybody from the director to the stars claimed to have thought up this piece of intimate business, but it had been included in Casey Robinson's script long before shooting. In fact, it occurred much earlier in *The Rich Are Always With Us* (1932) wherein George Brent smoothly performs the same gesture with Ruth Chatterton in a bedroom scene. Incidentally, the 24-year-old Miss Davis played 'the pest of Park Avenue' in it.

In *All About Eve* (1950), Bette remarks that she 'detests cheap sentiment.' In a way, *Now, Voyager* celebrates it. But despite the sogginess and absurdities, the central love affair creates genuine emotion. As proof of this, Davis received piles of letters, many of them from plain, unhappy women who passionately identified with Charlotte, in a film where love proved more effective than any cosmetic surgery.

WITNESS
Harrison Ford and Kelly McGillis

WITNESS
Harrison Ford and Kelly McGillis

Directed by Peter Weir
Paramount, 1985

Witness testifies to a romance between two people, not only from different worlds but, in essence if not in fact, from different centuries. The film opens in the isolated Amish community in Pennsylvania in what could be taken for the 18th century, where the descendants of Swiss Anabaptists live without electricity, telephones, or cars. Their clothes are plain, even buttons betoken vanity. Their simple rural existence, and their pacifist and religious philosophy, contrast vividly with the complexities and violence of modern American urban life that is not far from them in miles. Suddenly, this private society is intruded upon by a man from the outside, bringing with him some of the malevolence they shun. He is a Philadelphia detective, wounded by a bullet, and is driven to take refuge during a murder investigation on the farm of an Amish man, his young widowed daughter, and her small son who witnessed the brutal crime.

Harrison Ford is the intruder and Kelly McGillis the widow. From the start there is an implicit attraction between them which grows as she nurses him tenderly back to health. Because of her upbringing, however, their feelings remain unexpressed. One night, while he repairs his car in the barn, a pop song drifts from the radio. To 'What A Wonderful World' by Herb Alpert, the man and the woman dance – spontaneously, instinctively, joyously – illuminated by the headlights. They circle each other, their lips almost touching.

There is sexuality as well as the forbidden music in the air. The tune seems to liberate something in her, but he hesitates to make the next, usual, move. They are interrupted by her father who rebukes them, telling his daughter to feel shame. Sensing no shame in herself, she replies defiantly that it is, in fact, he who should be ashamed.

The widow's complete lack of compunction is seen on an evening as a storm rages. She is sponging down her body, when the detective stands at the door and looks upon her nudity. In a moment of delicate intimacy, she stares ahead at him unabashed and unbashful. Finally, he drops his eyes, and the relationship continues chaste. Yet, later, seeing him outside, she symbolically takes off her cap, goes out towards him, and enjoys their one embrace in the evening light.

In the end, he leaves her to go back to the big city, while she remains, presumably to marry the young Amish farmer who had been courting her. 'He's going back to the world where he belongs,' says her father. One is left to ponder why a woman obviously in love with the stranger, who had been married, had travelled outside the community, and had stood up to her father, should have remained unquestioningly in her restrictive world. Nevertheless, the film displays a relationship which is rare in the contemporary cinema, communicating a mysterious magic by the withholding of physical expression from love and sexual attraction.

CAMILLE
Robert Taylor and Greta Garbo

CAMILLE
Robert Taylor and Greta Garbo
Directed by George Cukor
MGM, 1936

All of Greta Garbo's films focused on love and passion, often unhappy, as her sublime and incomparable beauty trapped her or her lovers in destruction. The love scenes best known to modern audiences, however, are from *Camille*, in which the star portrayed Marguerite Gautier, Alexandre Dumas' tragic courtesan. The wordly and cynical mistress of the arrogant Baron de Varville, Marguerite is transformed by her meeting with young Armand Duval (Robert Taylor) on whom her soulful eyes first alight at the opera. They fall passionately in love, but she is warned by Armand's father that whores do not make good wives, and that she will ruin his son's life and career if she marries him. And so she sacrifices the man she loves, as Eleanora Duse and Sarah Bernhardt had done on stage, and Nazimova (1921) and Norma Talmadge (1927) had on screen, before her. But it is Garbo who remains the supreme Lady of the Camellias. When Marguerite contracts tuberculosis, Armand hears about her illness and rushes to her bedside. Originally, director George Cukor filmed two death scenes, one with a long farewell speech and the other in which she speaks but little. Fortunately, the second was chosen – Garbo's face was eloquent enough. Armand swears never to leave her again. She smiles and, in the husky voice of the consumptive, says 'Perhaps it is better if I live in your heart – where the world can't see me.' A cough, a little shudder, her eyes open wide and she dies in his arms.

The very handsome Robert Taylor looked marvellous, but was completely eclipsed by the great star. As he said, 'I was a scared kid of 25 and she was 31, in full bloom, already a fantastic legend.' The legend had grown mainly from the three torrid romances she had made with John Gilbert, reflecting their real-life infatuation for each other. First came the heavily erotic and almost blasphemous *Flesh And The Devil* (1927) then, cleverly billed, 'Garbo and Gilbert in *Love*' the same year. After *A Woman Of Affairs* (1928) the talkies came in and Gilbert languished, appearing in only a few more films of little consequence, and none of them with Garbo.

When MGM were casting for *Queen Christina* (1933), Garbo vetoed their choice of Laurence Olivier and demanded the return of her old friend, Gilbert, to play Don Antonio. The ravishing Garbo, however, refused her co-star any passionate kisses as he had recently married Virginia Bruce, but the love scene between them in a room at an inn, when he discovers that the boy he is sharing it with is none other than the Queen of Sweden, was the high point of the picture. After making love before a raging fire, Garbo floats joyfully around the room, studying and touching the objects there. When he asks what she is doing, she replies, 'I have been memorising this room. In the future, in my memory, I shall live a great deal in this room.' Moviegoers have remembered the room and its lovely occupant ever since.

Camille

Queen Christina

FALLING IN LOVE
Robert De Niro and Meryl Streep

FALLING IN LOVE
Robert De Niro and Meryl Streep

Directed by Ulu Grosbard
Paramount, 1984

In the 40s, audiences raised handkerchiefs to their eyes as that very English couple, Celia Johnson and Trevor Howard, appropriately keeping their emotions firmly under control, parted from each other in *Brief Encounter* (1946) over cups of tea in a shabby railway station buffet. Their illicit but never-to-be-consummated love affair was played out amidst the humdrum activities of a small English country town, contrasting smartly with the highly-charged narration and Rachmaninov's richly romantic second piano concerto on the soundtrack. Similarly, almost four decades later, the blossoming affair between a very modern American couple, Meryl Streep and Robert De Niro, in *Falling In Love* was enacted at the coffee bar at Grand Central station, in the busy streets of Manhattan, and on the commuter train that brings them from Westchester to New York each morning. Both films construct telling juxtapositions of the romantic and the mundane, and both deal with the opposing forces of adultery and marriage, epitomized by trains and railway stations – significantly, places that symbolise transience, and where the everyday coexists with adventurous possibilities.

The Streep-De Niro couple, like the Johnson-Howard pair, lead the routine lives of ordinary middle-class people. They are happily married and successful in their careers, until Fate intervenes. In the British film, it is represented by a speck of dust that gets into Celia Johnson's eye on a railway platform and is removed by doctor Trevor Howard who happens to be there. Streep and De Niro are strangers on a train, both travelling every day, but without meeting. Chance throws them together in a book shop where they accidentally get their shopping bags mixed. They meet again regularly and, in spite of themselves, fall in love. But the bonds of convention prove too strong for them to consummate their relationship and they separate to return to their former lives. Nevertheless, their now-awakened desire cannot be stemmed, their marriages founder, and they recognise that they are forced to find each other again.

Strangely, in the post-sexual liberation, post-feminist era, *Falling In Love* has many of the attributes of the woman's picture of the 30s and 40s in which adultery cannot lead to gratification. In *Brief Encounter*, the audiences knew that there was no way the heroine would leave her husband for another man. Howard does the gentlemanly thing and goes off to Africa, while Johnson returns to the safety of her marriage. There is no such inevitability in the later film. Although it ends with the lovers embracing tenderly on the Westchester train, it hesitates on the brink of a happy ending. Both Streep and De Niro have friends caught up in the mad dance of marriage-adultery-divorce, as soul-destroying as a 'stable' marriage, but the charismatic playing of the stars is enough to convince the most cynical observer that love will find a way.

Brief Encounter (inset: *Falling In Love*)

HIGH SOCIETY
Bing Crosby and Grace Kelly

HIGH SOCIETY
Bing Crosby and Grace Kelly

Directed by Charles Walters
MGM, 1956

In a glittering Hollywood career lasting a mere five years, glamorous, glacial beauty Grace Kelly had been the love object of Gary Cooper, John Wayne, James Stewart, Ray Milland, Cary Grant, William Holden and Stewart Granger. In *High Society*, a Technicolor showcase for her patrician loveliness, she had a last fling romancing both Bing Crosby and Frank Sinatra, before taking on the real-life, royal role of Princess of Monaco. Just as *The Philadelphia Story* (1940) was tailor-made for the unique gifts of Katharine Hepburn, so the later musical remake was perfectly trimmed to fit Miss Kelly's classy image. And when Sinatra crooned to her 'You're Sensational', nobody disagreed.

As Tracy Lord, she was the priggish, stuck-up daughter of Rhode Island gentry about to marry stuffy and aristocratic George Kitredge (John Lund). But she hadn't reckoned with two unwelcome visitors – one was her ex-husband C. K. Dexter-Haven (Crosby), a popular composer, and the other Mike Connor (Sinatra), reporter on the unsavoury *Spy Magazine*, hoping to get exclusive coverage of the society wedding of the year. In the course of events, the carefree journalist melts 'the fair Miss Frigidaire', with his voice, unconventional attitude and plenty of champagne. The glowing closeups of Kelly show how much sensuality Sinatra had extracted from her, but it is in the tender scenes with Crosby, particularly, that she displays a hitherto unexplored warmth. This was undoubtedly aided by the fact that a genuine affection existed between the two, their having dated for a while, and even mooted marriage.

In a flashback, they sing 'True Love' in each other's arms on board the yacht of the same name. It was her first and last singing assignment and, though she never claimed to be a songstress, she did manage to carry the tune with poise. This touching scene makes their love and inevitable reconciliation credible. As critic Douglas McVay wrote, 'The duet emerges as one of the most persuasive illustrations of the power of song to convey sexual passion and affection more intensely than any exchange of spoken words or fervent embraces do'.

Just as Crosby and Sinatra were able to bring out some previously unseen aspects of Grace Kelly, so also had James Stewart and Cary Grant the skill to touch off Katharine Hepburn's most lovable traits in *The Philadelphia Story*. More so, even, than in her long partnership with Spencer Tracy, Hepburn was able to display her full range, (in her other three pictures with Grant, too) – tender and tough, intelligent and emotional – in other words, herself. Whereas Grace Kelly flounced prettily between her beaus, Hepburn set up more abundant sexual sparks at the centre of a sophisticated trio in the wittier, more effervescent earlier film. If the love scenes in its musical successor were like honey, then the ones in the 1940 version were like caviar.

The Philadelphia Story (inset: Kelly and Sinatra in *High Society*)

GONE WITH THE WIND
Clark Gable and Vivien Leigh

GONE WITH THE WIND
Clark Gable and Vivien Leigh

Directed by Victor Fleming
MGM, 1939

'I don't want the part for money, chalk or marbles', Clark Gable told producer David O. Selznick when he was offered the role of Rhett Butler in *Gone With The Wind*. Happily, he ate his words, and accepted $2,500 a week and $100,000 bonus. The handsome, macho 'King' of Hollywood was first choice for Rhett, but almost every female star of the day was considered for the wilful Scarlett O'Hara. A year later, when Selznick first saw the exquisite, green-eyed, 25-year-old English actress Vivien Leigh, the search was over and a famous coupling was born.

Despite the memorably spectacular moments of the movie, such as the burning of Atlanta, the huge party at 'Twelve Oaks', the ball, and the superb visual evocation of the Old South as represented by 'Tara', the O'Hara's immense white mansion, it was the central relationship between Rhett and Scarlett – a monument to devouring passion brilliantly embodied by Gable and Leigh – that lifted the film into the highest category. Both characters were spirited, arrogant, self-centred and amoral, in marked contrast to Ashley and Melanie Wilkes (Leslie Howard and Olivia de Havilland). Although Scarlett schemes to snare the fragile aristocratic Ashley, she is irresistibly drawn to the virile Captain Butler, roguish black sheep of a Charleston Family.

One of the most skilfully written, played and directed sequences deals with Rhett's proposal of marriage to the already twice widowed Scarlett. He is brief and to the point. 'I made up my mind that you were the woman for me, Scarlett, the first time I saw you at 'Twelve Oaks'. When she objects to this approach, he sinks down on one knee and takes her hand. 'It cannot have escaped your notice that for some time past the friendship I have felt for you has ripened into a deeper feeling. A feeling more beautiful, more pure, more sacred…dare I name it? Can it be love?' Although he is play-acting, there is much truth in what he expresses. When she tells him she will always love another man (Ashley), Rhett – in an assertion of masculinity that has thrilled millions – takes her in his arms, bends her head back and kisses her hard on the mouth again and again until she struggles for air. 'Rhett don't, I'll faint.' 'I want you to faint. This is what you were meant for, Scarlett.'

Naturally, the marriage of two such stubborn and tempestuous people is doomed. One night, when she calls him a drunken fool, he lifts her bodily and carries her up to their bedroom. In the end, when Rhett decides to leave her, she sobs, 'What's to become of me?' Turning in the doorway he replies , in one of the cinema's most well-remembered lines, 'Frankly, my dear, I don't give a damn.' Audiences over four-and-a-half decades, however, have given more than a damn for what probably remains the most popular and successful motion picture of all time.

TOP HAT
Fred Astaire and Ginger Rogers

TOP HAT
Fred Astaire and Ginger Rogers

Directed by Mark Sandrich
RKO, 1935

Fred Astaire and Ginger Rogers, the greatest dance duo in motion pictures, made nine glittering black-and-white RKO musicals between 1933 and 1939. His classy coolness and her brash ardour complemented each other perfectly, a seductive harmony which was counterpoised by the matching sensuous whiteness of her flowing dresses, and the sombre black sheen of his tuxedo. Their collusive interaction made their duets seem like mini-dramas in which all the mutual attraction, antagonism and romance of a relationship was enacted in dance, symbolic expressions of love-making. But the duets were not only gems studding the unscintillating stories – they traced the emotional development of the two characters.

Astaire and Rogers first two-stepped their way into the dance hall of fame in *Flying Down To Rio* (1933) with 'The Carioca', a samba requiring the partners to press their foreheads together. Two years after dancing head to head, they were dancing 'Cheek To Cheek' in *Top Hat*, a number that epitomized their brilliant duets. Although the tedious plot of mistaken identity did everything it could to keep them apart, the *raison d'être* of the film was to bring them together on the dance floor. This happened three times during the course of true love running rough and smooth. The first duet in the movie was one of a lively, flirtatious and competitive nature performed in a band stand in a park where, as the song goes, 'Isn't It A Lovely Day To Be Caught In The Rain?' In the 'Piccolino' finale, they gave an extraordinary exhibition of ballroom dancing to the gathered throng of revellers in a dazzlingly white imagined Venice at carnival time. While dancing to Irving Berlin's 'Cheek To Cheek', Fred seduces Ginger. He woos her with delicate hand passes, she rejects him by swirling away, he draws her to him and she capitulates. The smoochy duet works up to a climax and ends on a gentle, satisfied note. Ginger flops onto a seat, her face glowing with fulfilment. Fred gazes on her adoringly. Then, suddenly realizing what has happened, she slaps his face. Holding his cheek, Fred exclaims, 'She loves me!'

A lithesome, lilting *pas de deux* of a similar nature was 'Night And Day' from *The Gay Divorcee* (1934), after which Ginger again sinks down exhausted onto a seat, and Fred mops his brow. The number has shown them to be ineffably in love. one of the most haunting and passionate of duets, 'Never Gonna Dance' from *Swing Time* (1936), takes place in a deserted nightclub. In the plot, Fred is about to lose her to another man. He tries to hold Ginger close to him but she achingly swings away from him, and the number ends in separation. Of course, they are reunited for the joyous finale. However, different career interests did force Astaire and Rogers to go their separate ways after *The Story Of Vernon And Irene Castle* (1939), nostalgically reuniting only once, a decade later, in *The Barkleys Of Broadway* (MGM).

The Gay Divorcee (inset: *Top Hat*)

KING KONG
Kong and Jessica Lange

KING KONG
Kong and Jessica Lange

Directed by John Guillermin
Paramount, 1976

'And the Beast looked upon the things of Beauty and lo! his hand was stayed from killing and from that day forward he was as one dead.' The Arab proverb openly states the theme at the beginning of *King Kong* (RKO, 1933). The Beast, a 50-foot high gorilla, and Beauty, raven-haired Fay Wray, formed the most unlikely romantic pairing in movie history. She is part of an expedition to Skull Island, near Sumatra. Earlier, dressed in a medieval robe, auditioning for a possible role in the movie of the adventure, the director tells her, 'Scream, Ann, scream for your life!' She does so, as if she has a premonition of the dangers to come.

Kong first claps eyes on her after she has been chained between two pillars by the natives of the island as a sacrifice to appease him. Obviously entranced, he examines her closely, picks her up in his gigantic hand, and takes her off with him into the jungle. Placing his captive gently down on a tree trunk, he proceeds to fight off prehistoric monsters. The enamoured ape takes the screaming, half-clad Miss Wray in his palm and begins to peel off her clothes like a banana. There has been speculation ever since, facetiously hinted at in the 1976 remake, of what would have happened if the creature had not been interrupted in his advances, and she had given in. Nevertheless, Kong was the most tremendous, if bizarre, suitor any film actress ever had.

Fray Wray explained. 'Mr Cooper (Merian C. Cooper, the co-producer co-director) said to me that he had an idea for a film in mind. The only thing he'd tell me was that I was going to have the tallest, darkest leading man in Hollywood. Naturally, I thought of Clark Gable.' In fact, Miss Wray didn't have much chance to get to know her colossal co-star. In their scene together in the jungle, she was filmed separately, her clothes being pulled off by wires, carefully lit so as not to appear in the shot. Then, with a brilliant use of back projection, she and Kong made physical contact.

The later colour version updated the fairy tale to the 70s, treating the sexual undertones of the original with a more obviously knowing air. However, the ape was still seen in full-frontal nudity without any visible means of procreation. Former model, blonde Jessica Lange was no screamer in the Fay Wray mould, but an urban swinger. When Kong has washed her in a jungle waterfall, and begins to pick at her bra, she shouts 'You goddamned male chauvinist ape!' But her initial horror turns to affection, whereas the earlier Kong mysteriously won audiences' affections, despite Fay Wray's undiminishing revulsion. His death, too, as he falls from the Empire State Building, was far more affecting in place and manner than the 1976 Kong's fall from the architecturally less interesting World Trade Centre. The moving epitaph spoken at the end, 'It was Beauty killed the Beast', was for the irreplaceable duo of King Kong and Fay Wray.

The 1933 RKO production (inset: the 1976 remake)

WUTHERING HEIGHTS
Laurence Olivier and Merle Oberon

WUTHERING HEIGHTS
Laurence Olivier and Merle Oberon

Directed by William Wyler
United Artists, 1939

When Victorian Gothic meets Hollywood Gothic the effect is usually a wildly romantic, glossy melodrama, of which one of the best examples was *Wuthering Heights*. The scriptwriters, concentrating purely on the passionate love story enacted by the brooding, darkly handsome Laurence Olivier as Heathcliff and Merle Oberon, the English beauty with the exotic features, as Cathy, eliminated much of Emily Bronte's classic novel. What emerged was the tale of how childhood affection between the daughter of the manor and the gypsy boy grows into a love that endures even beyond the grave.

Producer Sam Goldwyn was initially against the project saying, 'I don't like stories with people dying in the end. It's a tragedy'. Director William Wyler talked him into it, saying that Warners were interested in making it with Bette Davis. Wyler also had to fly to England to convince Olivier to take the role. The British actor, who was living discreetly with Vivien Leigh (both were still married to others), didn't want to leave her behind. So Wyler offered her the smaller role of Isabella. Vivien, who wanted to play Cathy or nothing, refused. 'Look, Vivien,' Wyler told her, 'you're not known in the States, and you may become a big star, but for the first role in an American film you'll never do better than Isabella.' Leigh was adamant but accompanied Olivier to Hollywood anyway – where she soon proved Wyler wrong by landing the role of Scarlett O'Hara in *Gone With The Wind*!

To capture the atmosphere of the all-important Yorkshire moors of the novel, acres of heather were shipped to the California hills, and wonderfully craggy sets were designed, as background to the tempestuous relationship which culminates in Cathy's premature death. Olivier poignantly displays Heathcliff's divine anger as he pushes his way into Cathy's bedroom and, exclaiming 'Leave her alone – she's mine', cradles the dead girl in his arms and weeps. To satisfy Goldwyn's need for a happy ending, a final scene reunited the ghosts of Heathcliff and Cathy, walking near Peniston Crag where they had spent their happiest hours.

A year later, Olivier portrayed another brooding hero in Alfred Hitchcock's *Rebecca*, a vivid version of Daphne Du Maurier's mock Gothic novel in which a vast Cornish mansion holds past secrets. Opposite him was the budding blonde actress Joan Fontaine. In a similar role, Fontaine was cast as the put-upon governess in the 1944 moody film adaptation of Charlotte Bronte's *Jane Eyre*. Though less romantic than *Wuthering Heights*, nor as passionate, there was an intriguing contrast between Orson Welles' glowing larger-than-life Edward Rochester and the gentle, sensitive Fontaine. In the final tender scene, when Rochester is maimed and blinded by the fire that ruined Thornfield Hall, his need for Jane's love is greater than ever before and, as in all great love stories, she has the capacity to give it.

DOCTOR ZHIVAGO
Omar Sharif and Julie Christie

DOCTOR ZHIVAGO
Omar Sharif and Julie Christie

Directed by David Lean
MGM, 1965

Love stories in the cinema are invariably seen as intimate affairs played out in drawing rooms and bedrooms. But there are also those that take place against a background of the great historical events that can impinge upon romantic attachment. The best, however, focus on both private and public agonies. Vivien Leigh and Clark Gable are thrown together as the American Civil War rages in *Gone With The Wind* (1939). Gary Cooper and Helen Hayes in 1932, and Rock Hudson and Jennifer Jones in 1957, lived out *A Farewell To Arms*, Hemingway's poignant World War I romance, while, among the many lovers torn asunder by World War II, Robert Taylor and Vivien Leigh in *Waterloo Bridge* (1940) stand out; against the immense backdrop of the Napolenoic Wars, the Hollywood version of *War And Peace* (1956) managed to bring out the tragic story of Natasha (Audrey Hepburn) and Andrei (Mel Ferrer). Revolutionary Russia controlled the fates of John Reed (Warren Beatty) and Louise Bryant (Diance Keaton) in *Reds* (1981), and was the setting for *Doctor Zhivago*.

'David Lean's *Doctor Zhivago* does for snow what his *Lawrence Of Arabia* did for sand,' wrote American critic John Simon on its release. Tons of simulated snow covered acres of ground in Spain where it was shot, through which a very un-Russian cast trudged. Yet much of the film had the feel of Russia, where the central doom-laden love affair is enacted.

In the title role, Omar Sharif, heart-throb of the Egyptian cinema, used his melting brown eyes to express the melancholy of the poet-doctor hero. As Lara, the object of his adoration, Julie Christie, with the British New Wave image still clinging to her, brought a certain modernity to the role. Just as Maurice Jarre's popular 'Lara's Theme' runs through the film's Oscar-winning score, so Zhivago's relationship with Lara weaves its way like a golden thread through the spectacular tapestry of war and revolution.

Yuri Zhivago, a medical student in Moscow, meets Lara, the beautiful daughter of a dressmaker, several times, but she first makes a deep impression on him after she has shot a man who tried to rape her. Their respective marriages separate them, but the Great War brings them together again, when she is a nurse at the front. Apart once more, her features are in his mind as he composes his poetry. Looking through the ice crystals forming on the window pane, he sees flower petals and Lara's face in closeup. Deserting from the Red Army, he attempts to make his way to her across the snowy steppes – it is not only events that keep them apart, but the vast Russian landscape, evoked in Panavision 70.

Boris Pasternak's Nobel Prize winning novel expressed the belief that humanity is controlled by the sweep of destiny. The film depicts humanity on a massive scale through the observation of the tempest-tossed lovers.